7 STEPS TO ACHIEVING WORK-LIFE BALANCE

B. VINCENT

---

7 STEPS TO ACHIEVING WORK-LIFE BALANCE

A MODERN GUIDE

QuillQuest Publishers

CONTENTS

INTRODUCTION

During a time where the lines among work and life obscure more as time passes, finding balance has turned into a vital mission for people looking for satisfaction, efficiency, and bliss. "7 Moves toward Accomplishing Balance between serious and fun activities: A Cutting edge Guide" is created as your compass in exploring the mind boggling territory of current obligations, yearnings, and individual prosperity.

The Quintessence of Equilibrium

At its center, balance between serious and fun activities encapsulates the congruity between our expert responsibilities and individual life, a concordance that permits us to accomplish our objectives without forfeiting our wellbeing, connections, or self-improvement. This equilibrium isn't about equitably conveying hours among work and recreation yet about accounting for what makes the biggest difference in our lives, guaranteeing that outcome in one region doesn't prompt disregard in another.

The Advanced Test

The advanced period has carried with it unmatched accommodations and open doors, yet it has additionally presented new difficulties in keeping up with balance between serious and fun activities. The consistent availability, the strain to be dependably "on," and the quick speed of progress have made it progressively hard to disengage, to rest, and to focus on our prosperity. In the midst of these difficulties, the journey for balance has become more significant than any time in recent memory, for our singular wellbeing and satisfaction as well as for the manageability of our social orders and economies.

The Misinterpretations

Numerous fantasies encompass balance between serious and fun activities, from the thought that it is an extravagance managed exclusively to a couple, to the possibility that it implies having everything. One of the most widely recognized confusions is the confidence in a one-size-fits-all arrangement. Be that as it may, accomplishing balance is profoundly private and continually advancing, mirroring our special qualities, conditions, and stages throughout everyday life. Perceiving and exposing these fantasies is the most vital move toward understanding and accomplishing genuine equilibrium.

The Reason for This Aide

This guide is intended to explore the intricacies of present day work and life, offering pragmatic systems, bits of knowledge, and activities that can prompt a more adjusted presence. Through the seven stages framed in the accompanying sections, we will investigate how to evaluate your present status, put forth significant objectives, focus on successfully, put down and regard stopping points, embrace adaptability, oversee pressure, and ceaselessly adjust to keep up with balance as your life advances.

Setting out on the Excursion

The excursion to accomplishing balance between serious and fun activities is continuous and dynamic. It requires tolerance, reflection, and steadiness. As you turn the pages of this aide, recollect that equilibrium isn't an objective however a way of voyaging. Each step moved toward a seriously satisfying life, where work and individual life exist together as well as improve each other.

In the sections that follow, we will dive into every one of the seven stages, outfitting you with the information, apparatuses, and certainty to leave on this excursion. We should start.

CHAPTER 1: UNDERSTANDING WORK-LIFE BALANCE

In our quest for progress and satisfaction, we frequently wind up shuffling the requests of our expert vocations and individual lives. This sensitive demonstration of adjusting work and life is an idea that has dazzled society's consideration, particularly as the limits between the two domains become progressively interlaced. In any case, what precisely is balance between fun and serious activities, and for what reason is it so significant in our cutting edge time? This part looks to uncover these responses, offering bits of knowledge into the embodiment of equilibrium, its authentic development, and the contemporary difficulties that entangle its accomplishment.

Characterizing Balance between serious and fun activities

Balance between serious and fun activities alludes to the condition of harmony where an individual similarly focuses on the requests of one's profession and the requests of one's very own life. In any case, the effortlessness of this definition gives a false representation of the intricacy of its application. Balance doesn't suggest an equivalent parceling of time but instead the fulfillment of a wonderful degree of coordination among work and individual exercises. This equilibrium is emotional, fluctuating incredibly among people contingent upon their jobs, values, and life stages.

The Development of Balance between fun and serious activities

The idea of balance between serious and fun activities isn't static; it has developed essentially after some time, formed by social movements, monetary changes, and innovative progressions. In the early modern time, work and life were frequently genuinely and transiently particular. Nonetheless, as economies and social orders have grown, particularly with the appearance of computerized innovation, the lines among work and individual life have obscured. The all day, every day network made conceivable by the web and cell phones has decisively changed how and when we work, testing customary ideas of equilibrium.

The Advanced Difficulties

Accomplishing balance between serious and fun activities in the cutting edge world is loaded with difficulties. The ascent of the "consistently on" work culture has prompted longer working hours and the disintegration of clear limits among work and individual time. Also, cultural assumptions regarding profession achievement and individual satisfaction have strengthened, putting extra strain on people to succeed in each part of their lives.

Globalization and the serious work market have likewise added to work-life clashes, with people frequently wanting to forfeit individual chance to satisfy work needs. Besides, the new shift towards remote work, while offering adaptability, has additionally obscured the lines among work and home, making it much more challenging to isolate the two.

Why Balance between fun and serious activities Matters

The mission for balance between fun and serious activities is in excess of an individual undertaking; it has significant ramifications for our prosperity, connections, and society at large. Accomplishing a good arrangement can prompt superior mental and actual wellbeing, higher efficiency and occupation fulfillment, and more grounded individual connections. On the other hand, unfortunate balance between fun and serious activities can bring about pressure, burnout, and a large group of medical problems, influencing the person as well as the working environment and local area.

Besides, balance between fun and serious activities is progressively perceived as a critical figure drawing in and holding ability, with numerous people esteeming adaptability and equilibrium as much as, while perhaps not more than, pay and advantages. This shift highlights the requirement for people and associations to focus on and effectively seek after balance between fun and serious activities.

Understanding balance between serious and fun activities is the most important phase in accomplishing it. By perceiving the intricacies, difficulties, and significance of equilibrium, we can start to make informed moves towards coordinating our work and individual lives in a manner that advances our general prosperity and satisfaction. The ensuing parts will investigate useful procedures and moves toward explore this excursion towards accomplishing an agreeable equilibrium.

CHAPTER 2:
SELF-ASSESSMENT AND GOAL SETTING

Accomplishing an agreeable balance between fun and serious activities starts with an exhaustive self-evaluation and the setting of clear, feasible objectives. This section investigates the significance of understanding your ongoing circumstance and how to successfully put forth objectives that will direct you towards a more healthy lifestyle.

The Significance of Self-Evaluation

Self-evaluation is the most common way of searching internally to comprehend your present status of balance between serious and fun activities. It includes inspecting your everyday schedules, work propensities, individual life, and generally prosperity to recognize areas of fulfillment and regions requiring improvement. This reflective cycle is essential for perceiving the hole between your present status and where you need to be.

Leading Your Self-Appraisal

Begin your self-evaluation by asking yourself key inquiries about your work and individual life. Consider:

·How long do you commit to function every week? Does this allow for individual exercises, connections, and rest?

·Do you feel anxious or overpowered by your work or individual obligations?

·How fulfilled would you say you are with your ongoing degree of efficiency and imagination at work?

·Do you have side interests or exercises that you routinely participate in beyond work?

·How might you depict your physical and psychological well-being?

Considering these inquiries can assist with featuring regions where your balance between fun and serious activities might be slanted.

Recognizing Regions for Development

When you have a more clear comprehension of your ongoing circumstance, the following stage is to recognize explicit regions for development. This could mean lessening work hours, devoting additional opportunity to loved ones, getting another side interest, or zeroing in on wellbeing and health.

Laying out Shrewd Objectives

With regions for development distinguished, now is the ideal time to lay out objectives. Utilizing the Shrewd models — Explicit, Quantifiable, Feasible, Significant, and Time-bound — can make your objectives more unmistakable and attainable. For instance:

·Explicit: I will commit two hours consistently to continuous quality time with my loved ones.

·Quantifiable: I will decrease my work hours from 60 to 50 hours out of each week.

·Attainable: I will plan three exercise center meetings each week to work on my actual wellbeing.

·Applicable: I will allot 30 minutes every day to care practices to upgrade my psychological prosperity.

·Time-bound: I will accomplish these changes inside the following three months.

Executing Your Objectives

Executing your objectives requires arranging and responsibility. Begin little, zeroing in on each or two objectives in turn, and step by step consolidate more as you change. Consistently survey your objectives and headway, making changes on a case by case basis. Keep in mind, accomplishing balance between serious and fun activities is an excursion, and it's OK to alter your objectives as your conditions change.

Self-appraisal and objective setting are central stages in your excursion towards accomplishing balance between serious and fun activities. By genuinely assessing what is happening and laying out Brilliant objectives, you can make a guide for a more adjusted and satisfying life. The following sections will dive into techniques for focusing on errands, overseeing time successfully, and defining limits, all of which will assist you with accomplishing the objectives you've set in this part.

CHAPTER 3: PRIORITIZATION AND TIME MANAGEMENT

In the mission for balance between serious and fun activities, successful prioritization and using time effectively are vital. This section investigates methods and techniques to assist you with focusing on your undertakings and deal with your time proficiently, guaranteeing that you can meet your expert obligations while additionally setting aside a few minutes for special goals and unwinding.

Figuring out Prioritization

Prioritization includes distinguishing the assignments that are generally significant and critical, and designating your time and assets as needs be. It's tied in with perceiving that not all assignments are made equivalent and that zeroing in your endeavors on the main thing can prompt more prominent productivity and fulfillment.

The Eisenhower Grid

One helpful instrument for prioritization is the Eisenhower Lattice, which orders errands into four quadrants in light of direness and significance:

·Quadrant 1: Assignments that are both pressing and significant. These ought to be done right away.

·Quadrant 2: Undertakings that are significant however not dire. These are fundamental for long haul achievement and ought to be booked.

·Quadrant 3: Undertakings that are dire yet not significant. These can frequently be designated.

·Quadrant 4: Undertakings that are neither dire nor significant. These ought to be limited or wiped out.

Utilizing this grid can assist you with zeroing in on errands that line up with your objectives and add to your balance between serious and fun activities.

Time Usage Methods

Powerful using time productively permits you to take advantage of your day, giving you command over your work and individual life. A few methods can help:

The Pomodoro Procedure

This procedure includes working for a set period (generally 25 minutes), trailed by a brief break. After four cycles, enjoy some time off. This can improve center and forestall burnout.

Time Impeding

Distribute explicit blocks of time for various exercises or undertakings over the course of your day. This guarantees that you commit time to both work and individual exercises, making your timetable more unsurprising and reasonable.

Restricting Performing various tasks

While performing various tasks could appear to be proficient, it frequently prompts diminished efficiency and nature of work. Zeroing in on each errand in turn can prompt improved results and less pressure.

Defining Limits

A fundamental piece of using time productively is defining limits to safeguard your time. This could mean setting explicit work hours, restricting night-time correspondence, or booking continuous time for leisure activities and unwinding. Conveying these limits to associates, companions, and family is vital.

Embracing Adaptability

While structure is significant, adaptability is as well. Unforeseen errands and open doors will emerge, and the capacity to adjust your timetable while keeping an emphasis on your needs is vital to dealing with these difficulties without forfeiting balance.

Prioritization and using time effectively are not tied in with getting more into your day; they're tied in with doing what makes the biggest difference productively and successfully. By utilizing these methodologies, you can gain significant headway towards your expert objectives while likewise cutting out time for individual satisfaction and unwinding.

In the following section, we'll investigate how defining limits and figuring out how to say no are basic for safeguarding your time and guaranteeing that your needs line up with your objectives for balance between serious and fun activities.

CHAPTER 4: SETTING BOUNDARIES AND SAYING NO

Accomplishing balance between serious and fun activities frequently requires a fragile discussion of significant investment between our expert and individual lives. Vital to this discussion is the capacity to define limits and serenely say no. This section dives into the significance of limits, techniques for setting them, and the craft of declining demands without culpability.

The Significance of Limits

Limits are the cutoff points we set to safeguard our time, energy, and prosperity. They empower us to isolate our work and individual lives, guaranteeing that neither infringes a lot on the other. By laying out clear limits, we can lessen pressure, forestall burnout, and work on our general personal satisfaction.

Perceiving the Requirement for Limits

The most vital phase in defining limits is perceiving the requirement for them. Signs that you might have to define more grounded limits incorporate inclination overpowered, angry of your work or individual responsibilities, or on the other hand assuming you find your work seeping into your own time consistently.

Methodologies for Defining Limits

Defining limits requires mindfulness and clear correspondence. Here are a few methodologies to lay out and keep up with limits really:

·Characterize Your Cutoff points: Obviously recognize what you are willing and not ready to acknowledge in both your work and individual life. Think about your needs, values, and the equilibrium you expect to accomplish.

·Impart Plainly: Whenever you've laid out your limits, convey them obviously and confidently to your associates, companions, and family. Be immediate however conscious in your correspondence.

·Be Predictable: Consistency is critical to keeping up with limits. Maintain your limits by reliably applying them, in any event, while it's difficult.

·Figure out how to Say No: Saying no is a vital part of keeping up with limits. Work on expressing no to demands that contention with your needs or would think twice about balance.

The Craft of Saying No

Saying no can be troublesome, particularly in the event that you're accustomed to taking on numerous obligations or are stressed over disheartening others. In any case, saying no is fundamental for safeguarding your time and prosperity. Here are a few ways to say no successfully:

·Be Immediate however Courteous: Obviously express your powerlessness to take on the solicitation. You can be amiable without offering pointless avocations.

·Offer Other options: If conceivable, offer other options or propose another person who could possibly satisfy the solicitation.

·Stand Firm: Individuals might push back when you say no. Be ready to repeat your position tranquilly and immovably.

Defining limits and figuring out how to say no are essential abilities for anybody trying to accomplish balance between serious and fun activities. By laying out limits and safeguarding your time, you can guarantee that your work and individual life are as one. Keep in mind, defining limits isn't tied in with restricting yourself yet about enabling yourself to zero in on the main thing.

In the following part, we will investigate the significance of embracing adaptability and assignment, further systems to keep up with balance in the midst of the requests of present day life.

CHAPTER 5: EMBRACING FLEXIBILITY AND DELEGATION

As we continued looking for balance between fun and serious activities, inflexibility can be our most exceedingly terrible foe. Life is intrinsically erratic, and our arrangements frequently need to adjust to unforeseen changes. This section examines the significance of embracing adaptability in our way to deal with work and life, close by the critical job of designation in dealing with our obligations productively.

The Worth of Adaptability

Adaptability permits us to adjust to life's unpredictabilities without neglecting to focus on our balance between serious and fun activities objectives. It includes being available to changing how and when undertakings are finished, taking into consideration a more responsive and less upsetting way to deal with both work and individual responsibilities.

Adaptability in Work Planning

For the majority, the conventional all day typical working day is becoming old. Adaptable work plans, like adaptable hours, working from home, and compacted work filled weeks, can assist people with fitting their plans for getting work done to more readily accommodated their own lives. This adaptability can prompt expanded work fulfillment, efficiency, and generally speaking prosperity.

Adaptability in Private Life

Likewise, being adaptable in our own lives — whether it's changing plans with companions or family, or moving individual ventures — can assist us with better dealing with our time and lessen pressure. It's tied in with tracking down balance in the smoothness of life, as opposed to sticking rigorously to pre-set plans.

The Craft of Designation

Assignment is one more key part in accomplishing balance between fun and serious activities. It includes relegating assignments to other people, saving time for undertakings that require your novel abilities or for individual exercises that add to your prosperity.

Assignment at Work

Numerous experts battle with assignment because of worries over loss of control or questions about others' capacities. Nonetheless, compelling designation can prompt more useful and drawn in groups, permitting you to zero in on high-need errands. Tips for powerful assignment include:

·Obviously impart task necessities and assumptions.

·Pick the ideal individual for the undertaking in light of abilities and responsibility.

·Trust your colleagues and offer help without continuously hovering over.

Assignment in Private Life

Assignment isn't restricted to the work environment. In our own lives, offering liabilities to relatives or re-appropriating undertakings can be similarly gainful. Whether it's isolating family errands, employing an expert for home upkeep, or looking for help from companions, designation can assist with overseeing individual obligations all the more effectively.

Embracing Change

Taking on an adaptable outlook and being available to designation requires a readiness to embrace change. It includes relinquishing the requirement for control and believing others, which can be testing in any case fulfilling.

Adaptability and appointment are fundamental techniques for dealing with the intricacies of current life and work. By embracing these methodologies, we can explore our obligations all the more really, decrease pressure, and draw nearer to accomplishing an agreeable balance between fun and serious activities. Keep in mind, the objective isn't to do it isolated however to find an equilibrium that considers both efficiency and individual satisfaction.

In the following section, we will investigate procedures for overseeing pressure and rehearsing taking care of oneself, further fundamental components in keeping up with balance between serious and fun activities.

CHAPTER 6: STRESS MANAGEMENT AND SELF-CARE

Pursuing harmony among serious and fun exercises, stress the board and dealing with oneself emerge as essential parts. The high level working environment, with its fast speed and high demands, can often provoke pressure, which, if not supervised true to form, can crumble both our master execution and individual thriving. This part offers encounters into understanding strain, methods for managing it, and the occupation of dealing with oneself in shielding balance among fun and serious exercises.

Sorting out Strain

Stress is a trademark response to demands put on us by our work, associations, and various strains. While a particular level of pressure can be rousing, unreasonable tension can provoke burnout, apprehension, and real ailments. Seeing the signs of pressure is the most fundamental stage in administering it.

Systems for Supervising Strain

Directing strain incorporates both proactive and responsive measures. Proactive measures consolidate setting sensible presumptions, zeroing in on endeavors, and staying aware of sound cutoff points. Open measures incorporate exercises you can take while feeling restless. The following are a couple of methods:

·Center around Your Flourishing: Standard action, good rest, and a sound eating routine are vital to directing strain.

·Care and Loosening up Methods: Practices like reflection, yoga, and significant breathing exercises can diminish sensations of nervousness and work on your sensation of success.

·Utilizing time actually: Useful utilizing time successfully can help with decreasing the vibe of being overwhelmed by work or individual tasks.

·Search for Help: Try to help from colleagues, family, or specialists when stress becomes unmanageable.

The Meaning of Dealing with oneself

Dealing with oneself is the demonstration of taking action to safeguard or work on one's own prosperity. It is a basic piece of strain the board and achieving balance among serious and fun exercises. Dealing with oneself can take many designs, from proactive undertakings that help your prosperity to practices that feed your soul and fulfillment.

Coordinating Dealing with oneself into Your Everyday practice

Coordinating dealing with oneself into your everyday timetable needn't bother with to be drawn-out or expensive. It will in general be basically pretty much as fundamental as getting a charge out of short respites throughout the day, participating in a side revenue, or concentrating on nature. The key is to make dealing with oneself a typical piece of your life.

Dealing with oneself Contemplations

·Genuine Dealing with oneself: Work-out reliably, eat quality meals, and get adequate rest.

·Significant Dealing with oneself: Keep a journal, practice appreciation, or partake in treatment or coordinating.

·Social Dealing with oneself: Contribute quality energy with loved ones, join a club or assembling with equivalent interests, or volunteer.

·Extraordinary Dealing with oneself: Partake in significant practices, think, or concentrate on nature.

Stress the chiefs and dealing with oneself are essential in the journey toward balance among fun and serious exercises. By getting it and having a tendency to pressure, and by zeroing in on dealing with oneself, you can defend your thriving and overhaul your ability to see the value in both your own and capable life.

In the accompanying segment, we will research the meaning of determined evaluation and change en route to achieving and staying aware of harmony among fun and serious exercises.

CHAPTER 7: CONTINUOUS EVALUATION AND ADJUSTMENT

The excursion to accomplishing and keeping up with balance between serious and fun activities is progressing, described by patterns of evaluation, activity, and correction. This last section underlines the significance of consistent assessment and the status to make changes as your conditions, needs, and objectives develop.

The Requirement for Ceaseless Assessment

Life is dynamic, loaded up with changes in private conditions, profession advances, and developing needs. What is balance at one phase in your life might appear to be extremely unique at another. Routinely assessing your balance between serious and fun activities guarantees that you stay lined up with your objectives and values, even as they change over the long run.

Techniques for Standard Appraisal

Persistent assessment includes occasionally returning to your objectives, needs, and the viability of your systems for accomplishing balance. Here are a few procedures to integrate this training into your life:

·Planned Audits: Put away opportunity month to month or quarterly to survey your advancement towards balance between serious and fun activities. Think about what's working, what's not, and what has changed in your life.

·Criticism Circles: Look for input from family, companions, and associates. They can give important viewpoints on your balance between serious and fun activities and propose regions for development.

·Changing Objectives: Be ready to change your objectives in light of your evaluations. Life's unconventionality might expect you to reclassify how equilibrium affects you.

Adapting

Whenever you've assessed your present status of balance between serious and fun activities, the subsequent stage is to make the vital changes. This could mean changing your time usage systems, defining new limits, or returning to your needs. Keep in mind, change is an indication of responsiveness to your life's necessities, not an inability to accomplish balance.

Embracing Change

Change is inescapable, and embracing it is vital to keeping up with balance between serious and fun activities. Remain open to better approaches for accomplishing balance and be adaptable in your methodology. In some cases, the best changes come from surprising changes or difficulties.

Remaining Resolved to Adjust

Keeping up with balance between fun and serious activities requires continuous responsibility and exertion. It's not difficult to return to old propensities, particularly during occupied or distressing times. Help yourself to remember the advantages of equilibrium for your prosperity, connections, and execution at work.

Ceaseless assessment and change are basic for accomplishing and supporting balance between serious and fun activities. By remaining focused on this interaction, you can explore the intricacies of present day existence with versatility and adaptability, guaranteeing that both your work and individual life remain satisfying and agreeable.

As we close this aide, recollect that balance between serious and fun activities is definitely not a one-time accomplishment yet a constant excursion. The systems and bits of knowledge partook in these sections are apparatuses to help you on this way. Embrace the excursion, remain adaptable, and continue moving towards a reasonable and remunerating life.

CONCLUSION

As we arrive at the finish of our excursion through "7 Moves toward Accomplishing Balance between serious and fun activities: A Cutting edge Guide," it's essential to ponder the pith of what we've investigated and the extraordinary way forward. Accomplishing balance between serious and fun activities is in excess of an objective; it's a consistent excursion of self-revelation, transformation, and development.

Embracing the Excursion

The mission for balance among work and life is a profoundly private undertaking, one that develops alongside our evolving needs, yearnings, and conditions. We've explored through understanding the significance of balance between fun and serious activities, the basic strides of self-appraisal and objective setting, dominating prioritization and using time productively, defining limits, saying no, embracing adaptability and designation, overseeing pressure, and focusing on taking care of oneself. Each step, a structure block, adds to an establishment whereupon a healthy lifestyle can be developed.

The Force of Persistent Assessment and Change

As highlighted in the last part, consistent assessment and change are significant. Life is unusual, and our requirements and needs shift. Routinely returning to our objectives, techniques, and limits permits us to adjust to these changes, guaranteeing that our journey for offset stays lined up with our actual selves.

The Gradually expanding influence of Equilibrium

Accomplishing balance between serious and fun activities accomplishes more than upgrade individual prosperity; it makes a far reaching influence that helps our connections, working environments, and networks. A healthy lifestyle empowers us to carry the best version of ourselves to each part of our reality, improving our own lives as well as everyone around us.

Pushing Ahead

As you push ahead, recollect that equilibrium is definitely not a one-time accomplishment yet a consistent course of arrangement and realignment. Be thoughtful to yourself, perceiving that flawlessness isn't the objective yet rather a significant, satisfying, and healthy lifestyle.

Allow this manual for be a beginning stage, a buddy on your excursion towards accomplishing and keeping up with balance between serious and fun activities. The means illustrated here are not direct however repetitive, intended to be returned to and updated as you develop and change.

Last Contemplations

All things considered, the way to balance between fun and serious activities is exceptionally yours to walk. A way of settling on decisions mirror your qualities, needs, and the sort of life you wish to lead. Embrace the excursion with liberality, adaptability, and sympathy for you and others.

May this guide act as a signal, enlightening the way towards a more adjusted, satisfied, and happy life.

www.ingramcontent.com/pod-product-compliance
Lightning Source LLC
Chambersburg PA
CBHW020522160726

47991CB00007B/3071